Robert Cogdell Gilchrist

The Confederate Defence of Morris Island, Charleston Harbor

Robert Cogdell Gilchrist

The Confederate Defence of Morris Island, Charleston Harbor

ISBN/EAN: 9783744761482

Printed in Europe, USA, Canada, Australia, Japan

Cover: Foto ©ninafisch / pixelio.de

More available books at **www.hansebooks.com**

THE

CONFEDERATE DEFENCE

OF

MORRIS ISLAND

CHARLESTON HARBOR,

BY THE

TROOPS OF SOUTH CAROLINA, GEORGIA AND NORTH CAROLINA,

IN THE

LATE WAR BETWEEN THE STATES,

WITH A MAP OF MORRIS AND PART OF FOLLY ISLANDS,
AND A PLAN OF FORT WAGNER.

Prepared from Official Reports and other sources

By MAJ. ROBERT C. GILCHRIST.

A PARTICIPANT, COMMANDING THE GIST GUARD ARTILLERY IN THAT DEFENCE.

[FROM THE YEAR BOOK—1884.]

CONFEDERATE DEFENCE OF MORRIS ISLAND.

Skirting along ship channel, the main entrance into Charleston harbor, and thus commanding the only approach for large vessels to the city, is MORRIS ISLAND : forever prominent in the history of the United States for being the site of the Battery that fired the first shot in the war between the States: still later for giving to the world its first lesson in iron-clad armor: and more than all, for being the theatre of a defence of an earth-work more stubborn and brave, of a siege as memorable and bombardments the most formidable in the annals of war.

This Island is three and three-fourths miles long, and varies in width from twenty-five to one thousand yards. At its Northern extremity it is flat, and with the exception of a low line of sand hills is only two feet above high tide. Three-fourths of a mile from Cummings Point (where was situated Battery Gregg) the marsh on the West encroaches, leaving a narrow strip between it and the sea of twenty-five yards. Here was located the famed Fort Wagner.* About two thousand yards Southward thence commences a range of hills of various height, stretching to "Oyster Point," the Southern end of the Island forming a secure shelter for troops. The Island is composed of quartz sand, which has no cohesion, and weighs, when dry, eighty-six pounds to the cubic foot. To its power in resisting the penetration of shot, and when displaced of falling back again to the very spot it had occupied, is due the comparative invulnerability of the works erected on this Island, advantageous alike to its defenders and assailants.

STAR OF THE WEST BATTERY.

After Sumter had been occupied by Major Anderson and the United States troops under his command against orders,

*At West Point there are only two models of fortifications used for purposes of instruction to the Cadets in the art of attack and defence ; one of these is *Fort Wagner*, the other Sebastopol.

to prevent reinforcements or supplies being sent to this
garrison, a two gun battery was erected on the Island, about
fifty or seventy-five yards South from the spot afterwards
occupied by Fort Wagner. A detachment of Citadel
Cadets, under Professor (now Bishop) P. F. Stevens, manned
the guns, supported by the Charleston Zouave Cadets, Capt.
C. E. Chichester, and German Riflemen, Capt. Jacob Small,
as Infantry. The Vigilant Rifles, eighty strong, under Capt.
S. Y. Tupper, were stationed at the lower end of the Island to
dispute a landing. The Battery was of the simplest character.
Its armament, two 24-pounder siege guns " en barbette,"
without traverses or protection of any kind. It had been
built very hastily, so that the guns and gunners were entirely exposed. A broadside of light navy shell guns could
have disabled it, and the guns of Fort Sumter completely
commanded it.

A little after daylight, on the morning of the 9th January,
1861, the long roll was beat and the troops were got under
arms. In the horizon a steamer was descried coming over
the bar. Whether armed or unarmed no one knew ; but
the orders from Governor Pickens were positive to fire into
her and prevent her approach to Sumter. At 7.15 A. M.
she was within range of the Battery, and Major Stevens
sighted the guns. Cadet Haynesworth (afterwards a Lieutenant in the First South Carolina Regulars, and now a
lawyer in Sumter, S. C.,) held the lanyard of the right gun,
and at the command fired the FIRST HOSTILE SHOT OF THE
WAR. It fell across her bows. At this she ran up a large
United States garrison flag to her fore. As she did not
stop, other shots were fired as rapidly as the guns could be
served ; about six in all. She checked her speed and began
to turn at the fourth shot. Only three or four struck her,
doing no damage of any consequence, as the range was great
for 24-pounders.

During the firing Sumter ran out her guns, and many an
anxious eye was cast to the rear, expecting each moment to
see her belch forth a fire which would have annihilated
those who had thus dared to fire on the " Stars and Stripes."

In April the same act set ablaze the Northern heart ; but on the 9th January it fell still-born.

STEVENS' IRON BATTERY.

When it was determined to invest Fort Sumter and reduce it with artillery, among other batteries erected within reach, Col. Clem. H. Stevens, a Cashier in the Planters' and Mechanics' Bank of Charleston, devised and built at Cummings Point the first iron-clad armored fortification ever erected. Over heavy timbers he placed railroad T iron, laid at an angle of from forty to forty-five degrees.

Fort Sumter was distant one thousand three hundred and ninety yards. Behind this "slaughter-pen," as many called it, the Palmetto Guard, Captain G. B. Cuthbert, fought through the 12th and 13th of April, 1861, pouring a heavy fire into the gorge of Sumter, which replied with a severe but ineffectual fire from her heaviest guns. At the close of the engagement "Stevens' Battery" was almost intact, only an iron cove of port-hole being displaced and one gun dismounted. Not a man of its garrison was hurt. This astounding success established the value of iron armor, of which both sides in the internecine struggle were quick to avail themselves, and this experiment has revolutionized the navies of the world.

BRIGADIER-GENERAL R. S. RIPLEY.

If to one man more than another Charleston was indebted for her safety until Sherman knocked at her back door, that man was General Ripley. Though by birth a Northerner, he was one of the first to offer his sword for the defence of the State of his adoption, and to consecrate to her service his all of ability, zeal and time. At the time of the bombardment of Sumter in April, 1861, he commanded Fort Moultrie, and it was by the red-hot shot he threw into it, that its barracks were set on fire and its surrender compelled. For some reason he was not in favor with the powers that were in Richmond, and as in this category the General of the Department was also placed, he was compelled to rely mainly upon his own resources, cramped as they often were at critical moments by heavy drafts from the War Department. What he accomplished with the limited material of war and small force at his disposal was superhuman. The success that crowned his efforts was his only reward.

FOLLY ISLAND.

Next South of Morris Island, and separated from it by " Light-house Inlet " (four hundred yards wide), is Little Folly Island. The topographical features of the North end of this Island, bordering on the Inlet, gave to the enemy every facility for the concealment of his designs. The sand hills alone obscure the view from Morris Island, but these were covered with a heavy growth of scrubby trees, which ought to have been removed by the Confederates when they controlled this stragetic point. Failure to do so enabled the Federals, under their cover, to secretly place in battery forty-seven pieces of artillery, with two hundred rounds of ammunition for each gun, provided with suitable parapets, splinter-proof shelters and magazines, almost within speaking distance of the Confederate pickets, and undiscovered by several reconnoisances made just before the assault of July 10th. This battery on Little Folly Island was the prelude to the memorable siege of Fort Wagner, and rendered necessary the fearful sacrifice of life, with the lavish expenditure of treasure that followed its unmasking.

FAILURE TO FORTIFY SOUTH END OF ISLAND.

It has always been a vexed question on whom should rest the blame for the neglect of this stragetic point. There were mutual recriminations and much "bad blood" between those who were thought to be responsible for the success of the Federals on the 10th of July, which involved the destruction of Fort Sumter, and the long and bloody siege of Fort Wagner. But the truth is General Beauregard did not believe an attack would be made by this route, and was firmly persuaded the enemy would again essay an advance over James Island.* He, therefore, withdrew all the negro laborers from Morris Island to strengthen the fortifications elsewhere, leaving the Gist Guard and Matthewes Artillery to finish half completed Fort Wagner. And when General Ripley, on his own responsibility, and by his own Engineer, commenced to fortify the neighborhood of Lighthouse Inlet, he peremptorily commanded the work to stop. Later, when it was discovered that General Vogdes was doing some work—its extent unknown—on Folly Island, General Ripley again, with the tardy consent of General Beauregard, sent two companies of the First South Carolina Artillery, Capt. John C. Mitchell commanding, who, with the assistance of the Twenty-first South Carolina Volunteers, Colonel Graham, built among the sand hills of the South end of Morris Island nine independent one gun batteries, which were eventually to meet the concentrated fire of forty-seven guns in the masked Federal Batteries on Little Folly Island, and 8, 11 and 15-inch guns in the Monitors.

DEFENCE OF CHARLESTON.

As the "Cradle of Secession," it was the ambition of the United States troops, at the very commencement of the war, to be possessed of Charleston. Equally determined were the Confederates to hold it to the last extremity. The effort to take it by a land approach over James Island had failed at the battle of Secessionville, 16th June, 1862. Now, it became evident, by the concentration of iron-clads, gunboats and transports in the Stono and adjacent waters, that a combined land and naval attack would be attempted. Two lines were open to their approach—one by way of Sullivan's Island and the other by Morris Island. The former was defended by batteries of the most formidable character, extending from Breach Inlet on the North to the Cove on

---

*"The holding of the position was secondary to that of James Island, which must first be secured beyond peril, if possible, of surprise and capture." See General Beauregard, Vol. 2, p. 493.

the South, and also by Fort Moultrie (of Revolutionary fame), but Morris Island was almost unprotected.

FORT WAGNER.

A short time after the battle of Secessionville, Fort Wagner was commenced. Captains F. D. Lee and Langdon Cheves, of the Confederate States Engineer Corps, planned and built it. The position before described, about three-quarters of a mile to the South of Cummings Point, was selected for its site. Here the Island is about two hundred and fifty yards wide, bounded by Vincent's Creek on the West, and the ocean on the East. Immediately in front the marsh from Vincent's Creek setting in towards the ocean, narrows it to but thirty-three yards, and this marsh even at low tides makes an impassable barrier. A low line of sand hillocks skirting the beach serves as a partial protection from the fleet in the channel, back to Cummings Point.* The higher sand hills of the Island are distant to the South two thousand yards. The intervening ground being a narrow strip, bounded by the ocean on one side, and the marsh on the other, of alternating width, from twenty-five to forty yards at high tide, along which the sappers and miners had to build their approaches. Nature designed this spot for defence, and there is no other site on the Island equal to it. Its distance from Fort Sumter is two thousand seven hundred and eighty yards.

DIMENSIONS.

Fort Wagner was an enclosed earth-work, measuring within the interior slopes from East to West six hundred and thirty feet, and from North to South in extreme width two hundred and seventy-five feet. The sea face, measuring

---

* This describes this portion of the Island as it was in 1863. Now (1885) it is almost on a level with the sea. Vincent's Creek is filled up, and the marsh covered with the sand that formed the fort and hills ; not a vestige remains either of Wagner or the Federal approaches. The sea has cut through between the first and second parallels, dividing the Island into two. We would suggest that the smaller of these two islands be hereafter called Wagner Island.

along the interior crest two hundred and ten feet, contained a bomb-proof magazine twenty by twenty feet, forming a heavy traverse to protect the three guns North of it from the land fire. Behind this sea face, parallel with the beach, was the bomb-proof, thirty by one hundred and thirty feet within, which could not accommodate more than nine hundred men standing elbow to elbow and face to back (not fifteen hundred to sixteen hundred men, as Gen. Gilmore says), and this capacity was further reduced by cutting off more than one-third for the hospital. In fact, not more than three hundred could, or ever did, obtain shelter in it at one time. The land face was irregular with re-entering angles, measuring in the whole length six hundred feet, with chambers for five guns to sweep the land approach, separated by heavy traverses to protect the guns from enfilade fire of fleet. The Western portion of the battery was an enclosed parade ground, containing one acre. From the East face to the beach, protecting the sally-port and extending to high water-mark one hundred feet, was an outer work pierced for two guns to sweep the sea face. The front of the battery was guarded by a ditch, filled with water at high tide and retained by sluice gates. Towards the close of the siege this ditch was filled with "trous de loups" and boards armed with spikes.

About two hundred and fifty yards in front of Fort Wagner, just beyond the marsh, was a sand ridge, affording shelter for pickets and sharp-shooters, the scene of conflict on the nights of August 21st, 25th and 26th.

ARMAMENT.

When direct operations against Fort Wagner commenced on the 10th July, the fort was armed with the following guns: One 10-inch Columbiad, one 32-pounder smooth-bore, one 42-pounder carronade, two naval 8-inch shell guns, three 32-pounder carronades, two 32-pounder siege howitzers, two 12-pounder bronze howitzers and one 10-inch mortar.

2

GARRISON.

There were on Morris Island July 10th, nine hundred and twenty-seven men, Col. R. F. Graham, of the Twenty-first South Carolina Volunteers, in command; Lieut-Col. Jos. A. Yates, of the First South Carolina Artillery, as Chief of Artillery; Capt. C. E. Chichester, of the Gist Guard Artillery, commanding Fort Wagner (by right of seniority). Artillery companies: Gist Guard, Lieut. R. C. Gilchrist, and Matthewes Artillery, Capt. J. R. Matthewes. In Battery Gregg, at Cummings Point, was Capt. Henry R. Lesesne, of the First South Carolina Artillery, with his company. At the South end of the Island, defending the nine single batteries erected there to dispute landing from Folly Island, were Companies I and E, and a detachment of H (two hundred men), of the First South Carolina Artillery, Capts. John C. Mitchell (son of the Irish patriot) and J. R. Macbeth, and Lieut. H. W. Frost, and a detachment of fifty men of the First South Carolina Infantry under Capt. Chas. T. Haskell, and the Twenty-first South Carolina Volunteers (six hundred and twelve men) under Maj. G. W. McIver.

It will be well, also, to give Gen. Beauregard's available force in his department at this time: Infantry, five thousand two hundred and fifty-six; artillery, five thousand seven hundred and ninety-four; cavalry, four thousand three hundred and eighteen; grand total, fifteen thousand three hundred and eighteen; distributed in Florida, Georgia and South Carolina; and for the immediate defence of Charleston five thousand eight hundred and sixty-one, of all arms. Gen. Gilmore had for carrying on offensive operations, after leaving Hilton Head and other important points perfectly secure, ten thousand infantry, three hundred and fifty heavy artillery, six hundred engineer troops, twenty-eight pieces flying artillery, completely equipped and mounted; and the following guns: five 200-pounder rifled Parrotts, nineteen 100-pounder rifled Parrotts, twelve 30-pounder Parrotts siege, four 20-pounder Parrotts siege, eight pieces field artillery dismounted, twelve 13-inch S. C. Mortars, ten 10-inch siege mortars, five 8-inch siege mortars and three cochorn mortars. The entire effective force in South Carolina was seventeen thousand four hundred and sixty-three, officers and men inclusive. The force actually employed on Morris Island at one time did not vary much from eleven thousand five hundred men, aided by a powerful fleet of iron-clads. Opposed to them the Confederates never had on the Island more than one thousand six hundred and one men, and at times this force was reduced to less than one thousand, divided between Fort Wagner and Battery Gregg; nor could it in any emergency have been increased to any practical extent, on account of the limited transportation at command and the exposed landing at Cummings Point.

ENGAGEMENT OF APRIL 7TH.

Fort Wagner proposed to play a very important part in the historic attack of the iron-clads of the Federal fleet on Fort Sumter; but, as it is believed, was defeated through treachery. Some time before an iron boiler filled with one thousand pounds of powder, fitted with electrical appliances for exploding it, had been sunk in the channel, one mile and a half from and abreast of Wagner. The submarine cable stretched to the shore and lay within the fort. A system of triangulation from both Gregg and Wagner, marked by stakes driven in those batteries, determined its position, and for days the opportunity to use it against the fleet had been anxiously looked for. At noon on the 7th of April—a lovely spring day, the deep blue sky, without a cloud, reflected in the bay as smooth as glass—a movement was observed among the iron-clads. Soon after they advanced slowly in line of battle; the monitors Weehawken, Passaic, Montauk, Patapsco, Catskill, Nantucket, Nahant and Keokuk, with the New Ironsides bearing the pennant of Commodore Dupont.

At ten minutes past 3 P. M., Moultrie opened her batteries; immediately thereafter Fort Sumter, Battery Gregg, and all the iron-clads joined in the thundering chorus—

"The music of the spheres." The sea seethed as a boiling cauldron, as shot and shell, with the debris of fort and vessels, plunged into it. Amid this pandemonium Wagner stood silent, yet all within were nerved to the most intense excitement. The long looked for hour was at hand when one of those dreaded iron-clad monsters would be hurled into the air. The New Ironsides was singled out for destruction. One of the Signal Corps had been stationed at Battery Gregg, and another at Fort Wagner, each with keen eyes watching their respective lines of vision. At the electric key stood Capt. Langdon Cheves, with his eyes bent on both stations, so that as the flags waved in concert, indicating the fateful moment when the Ironsides should be over the torpedo, to apply the spark and do the deed. Slowly the Ironsides steamed around, delivering one terrific broadside after another. Ever and anon the flag would wig-wag on Gregg, but Wagner's was still; then that on Wagner, but Gregg's did not reply, and so it seemed that hours passed. The garrison intent and watching, hearts could almost be heard beating above the din of battle. At last both flags waved. Oh, the wild rush of hope and joy that overwhelmed them as they felt that their hour had come at last. The key was touched once and again. All looked breathlessly towards the doomed ship. There was no answering explosion. Unconscious of the danger she had escaped, she steamed on and delivered her broadsides until the action closed. It was said afterwards and believed that the "*expert*" who was charged with arranging the torpedo was a "Federal spy."

That afternoon the first blood was spilled in Fort Wagner. Through disobedience of orders and carelessness, an ammunition chest was exploded in the gun chamber of Lieut. Steadman of the Matthewes Artillery, killing three and wounding five men; also dismounting the 32-pounder.

COMMENCEMENT OF HOSTILITIES.

Unfortunately for the defence of Morris Island, the

Steamer "Ruby" (a blockade-runner) got aground four hundred yards from Folly Island, by the South entrance to the Light-house Inlet, while the batteries were being built to command this approach. The temptation was too strong for the needy "Confeds," and while they were busy wrecking her, the more diligent and wary Federals were employed in erecting their ten masked batteries not five hundred yards away. This gave a false security to the District Commander, who reports the fact to Gen. Beauregard as proof that the enemy were not in force on Folly Island.

The morning of the 10th of July, 1863, told a different story. Citizens in Charleston, six miles distant, were aroused from their slumbers at early dawn by a terrific cannonade. Forty-seven pieces of artillery, consisting of rifled guns, 20 and 30-pound Parrott's and 10-inch mortars, poured an incessant fire on the unfinished Confederate batteries that were intended to protect the South end of the Island. The monitors Catskill, Montauk, Nahant and Weehawken steamed up to within less than a mile and delivered, enfilade, their broadsides of 11 and 15-inch shot and shell, while four howitzer launches opened on the right. Under cover of this terrible bombardment, lasting over three hours—heard in Edgefield, one hundred and thirty miles away—the Ninth Maine, Third New Hampshire, Sixth and Seventh Connecticut, Forty-eighth New York and Seventy-sixth Pennsylvania, two thousand five hundred men, under Brigadier-General Strong, put out in small boats from Folly River, and landed on Oyster Point.

The brave artillerists fought with great determination, but their guns were soon disabled, and they and the remnant of Infantry were compelled to retire before the overwhelming force, sustaining a loss of two hundred and ninety-four, including sixteen commissioned officers, killed, wounded and missing. The Federals lost but fifteen killed and ninety-two wounded.

THE RETREAT.

It was not until capture was imminent that the few gal-

lant men remaining, who had sustained this terrific on-
slaught for three hours, fell back, disputing every inch of
ground. The four monitors steamed slowly along, as near
to the shore as the depth of water would permit, pouring
in their broadsides of shrapnell and shells. The Federals,
two thousand five hundred strong, deployed across the
Island, from shore to shore, and delivered a murderous fire.
Two companies of the Seventh Battalion South Carolina
Infantry, Lieutenant-Colonel Nelson (whole battalion two
hundred and sixty effectives), which had just landed on the
Island, arrived in time to cover the retreat. The enemy
advanced until they came within range of the heavy guns of
Fort Wagner, which opened rapidly with shot and shell,
stopping the pursuit. Falling back to the shelter of the
sand hills, the Federal troops rested for the remainder of
the day.

CAPTAIN LANGDON CHEVES.

At 9 A. M. the Federal forces were in possession of the
sand hills of Morris Island. The " Stars and Stripes " had
replaced the " Stars and Bars " on Colonel Graham's headquarters. The artillery garrison of Fort Wagner manned
the guns, and throughout the day engaged the four monitors, which took position a mile away, abreast of the fort.
Captain Cheves, son of the late Judge Cheves, to whose
engineering skill and untiring zeal Fort Wagner was to be
thenceforth famous in history, was sitting in his quarters
overwhelmed with grief at the tidings just brought to him
of the death of his nephew, Captain Chas. T. Haskell. But
as the sound of approaching battle grew louder, he roused
himself to action, and stepping across the threshold of his
door, towards one of the magazines, he was stricken to death
by a fragment of the first shell hurled at Fort Wagner. His
work lived after him fifty-eight days. An untold weight of
shot and shell could not destroy it. The heaviest artillery
of that day, which reduced the walls of Sumter to a shapeless mass, four thousand five hundred yards away, at less

than one-third the distance, made but little impression on
that monument of his genius and labor. It was not until
the long and laborious sap and mine of the highest engineering skill, commenced one thousand six hundred yards
away, had reached the very moat, that the fort, unimpaired
in strength, and having accomplished the work designed,
was evacuated without loss to its garrison. The names of
Fort Wagner and Cheves should forever be one and in
separable.

FIRST ASSAULT.

During the morning and evening of the 10th Morris
Island was reinforced by Nelson's Battalion, Seventh South
Carolina Volunteers, two hundred and sixty men, and Col
onel Olmsted's command of Georgia troops, detachments of
First, Twelfth, Eighteenth and Sixty-third Georgia Regi
ments, five hundred and thirty-four men ; these, with twenty
men of Company D, First South Carolina Infantry, Lieut.
Horlbeck ; seventy men of Companies E, H and I, First
South Carolina Artillery, Capt. John C. Mitchell ; two hundred remnant of Twenty-first South Carolina Volunteers,
the Gist Guard and Matthews Artillery, under Captain Chichester, in all one thousand two hundred men, constituted
the Confederate force. The garrison of Wagner was ordered
to be on the alert against an impending attack. The night
was passed in comparative quiet, the men resting at their
post, and the artillerists sleeping in the gun-chambers.
Four hours past midnight the pickets on the ridge caught
the sound of stealthy footsteps advancing over the soft
sand. The early gloaming of dawn hardly revealed the form
of the foe. Waiting only to make "assurance doubly sure,"
they opened a rapid fire, and thus gave signal to the vigilant garrison of Wagner. In a moment the South Carolin-
ians manned the guns and the right and right centre of the
ramparts. The Georgians guarded the left and left centre
of the works ; the Eighteenth Battalion occupied the Southeast bastion ; the First Georgia along the sea front to the

left; the Twelfth Georgia Battalion to the right, Colonel R. F. Graham in command.

Four companies of the Seventh Connecticut, under Lieutenant-Colonel Rodman, led the assault. So rapidly did they follow on the heels of the retreating picket force, they were at the crest of the sea face as the pickets were entering the sally port. Against the dark sky the dim outline of a human figure could just be discerned. Lieutenant R. C. Gilchrist, of the Gist Guard, in command of the company, challenged him to know if he was friend or foe. Quick as thought the man's gun was levelled, and a ball parted the Lieutenant's hair, the powder blinding his eyes. His 32-pounder, double-shotted with grape and cannister, belched forth a reply, the whole load passing through the man's body, cutting him in twain, his discharged rifle dropping in the battery. This became the signal for the blast of war. Instantly the whole battery was ablaze. The artillery opened with a murderous hail of grape and cannister, while the musketry poured forth in a steady roll, their balls sent like wind and rain in the face of the foe. As the light of day increased, and the smoke cleared away, the retreating columns of blue coats were seen making for the sand hills. The remnant of the forlorn hope of the Seventh Connecticut, who had sheltered themselves against the scarp during the terrific fire, now crawled in and surrendered themselves prisoners, one hundred and thirty, rank and file. General Strong, who commanded in person on the 10th and 11th, reports his losses in the two days four hundred and thirty-six, but three hundred and fifty wounded were carried to Hilton Head, and over one hundred were buried by the Confederates in front of Wagner, one hundred and thirty taken prisoners. The loss in Wagner was one officer, Capt. C. Werner, of the German Volunteers, of Savannah, and five men killed, and one officer and fifteen men wounded—twelve in all.

CHANGE IN GARRISON.

After their signal repulse on the morning of the 11th, the

Federals were busy strengthening their position on the Island. On the 12th General Beauregard called a Council of general officers to discuss the practicability of driving the Federals from Morris Island. It was considered that not less than four thousand men would be required to do it. More than that number could not be manœuvered. The enemy's works must be carried before daylight, otherwise the advance and attack would be exposed to the fire of the fleet. The limited means of transportation at hand did not permit as large a force to be put on the Island in one night and give time to allow an advance to the South end before daylight. Unwillingly the idea was abandoned. That opportunity was lost. Never after was there the slightest chance that victory would have crowned the effort. Each day one or more monitors took position abreast of Wagner, shelling that fort and Gregg more or less vigorously.

The Confederate force, which had done such arduous duty, were relieved by the Fifty-first North Carolina troops (six hundred and eighty-seven men), under Col. H. McKethan; detachments from Captains Buckner and Dixon's Companies of Sixty-third Georgia Artillery; Captains Tatem and Adams' Companies of the First South Carolina Infantry as Artillery; section of howitzers of DeSaussure Artillery, Captain DePass; section of howitzers, Blake's Artillery, Lieutenant Waties; Charleston Battalion, Lieutenant-Colonel P. C. Gaillard, and Thirty-first North Carolina troops, Lieutenant-Colonel Knight. Brigadier-General William Taliaferro relieved Colonel Graham in the command of the Island.

BOMBARDMENT.

For several days there had been evidences of a renewed attack by land and sea on Fort Wagner. All the Federal fleet disappeared from Stono on the 17th. The New Ironsides and several gunboats crossed the bar, and the forces were increased on the Island. In five days four powerful batteries had been erected, the nearest within one thousand three hundred and thirty yards of Wagner; the furthest one thousand nine hundred and thirty yards. The first mounted five 10-inch siege mortars, the second nine 30-pounder and four 20-pounder Parrott rifles, the third four 10-inch siege mortars, and the fourth five 8-inch siege mortars and two 30-pounder, six 10-pounder Parrott rifles, four 3-inch rifles and two Wiard rifles—in all thirty-six pieces.

About daylight on the 18th the Federal mortars commenced their practice, which they kept up at intervals until noon. The New Ironsides, the monitors Montauk, Catskill, Nantucket, Weehawken and Patapsco, the gunboats Paul Jones, Ottowa, Seneca, Chippewa and Wissahickon steamed in and took position abreast of Wagner. At 12 o'clock all the land and naval batteries opened a "*feu d' enfer*" upon the devoted work. For eight long hours it was as a continuous reverberation of thunder, peal followed peal in rapid succession. NINE THOUSAND SHELL WERE HURLED AGAINST WAGNER (twenty each minute). It ceased only when darkness came on, as its further continuance would have involved the slaughter of the assaulting column, but strange to tell, few within the fort were injured—eight killed and twenty wounded. The two North Carolina Regiments during the bombardment were kept under the shelter of the bomb-proof. The greater portion of the Charleston Battalion was stationed along the parapet of the work, under Colonel Gaillard, a position they gallantly maintained the whole day exposed to the fearful fire, while the remaining companies, under Captain Julius A. Blake, took shelter behind the sand hills in the rear, yet within call. The light field pieces were dismounted from their carriages and buried in the sand for protection.

At the commencement of the bombardment Wagner had delivered a sharp and severe fire against the fleet, but in a short time its land batteries were entirely silent, and those of the sea front were practically so.

PREPARATION FOR ASSAULT.

As it became evident that an attack on Fort Wagner would be made at dark, Battery Gregg and Fort Sumter made ready to fire over Wagner on the advancing columns, and the batteries on James Island to enfilade its face. General Hagood was ordered to be in readiness to support, or relieve, General Taliaferro, and the Thirty-second Georgia Regiment, Colonel Harrison, proceeded to the reinforcement of the garrison. On the part of the Federals, Brigadier-General Strong's Brigade was to lead the assault. It was composed of the Fifty-fourth Massachusetts, Colonel Shaw; the Sixth Connecticut Regiment, Colonel J. L. Chatfield; a Battalion of the Seventh Connecticut Regiment, Colonel Barton; the Third New Hampshire, the Forty-eighth New York Regiment, Colonel Jackson; the Ninth Maine Regiment, Colonel Emery, and the Seventy-sixth Pennsylvania Regiment, Colonel Strawbridge, and was to be supported by Colonel Putnam's Brigade, comprising his own regiment (the Seventh New Hampshire), Lieutenant-Colonel Abbott; the One Hundredth New York Regiment, Colonel Dandy; the Sixty-second Ohio Regiment, Colonel Pond, and the Sixty-seventh Ohio Regiment, Colonel Voris. Brigadier-General T. Seymour to command the assaulting column, and to arrange details for attack.

Sometime before sunset these regiments were formed on the beach in rear of their batteries, in columns of eight companies, closed at half distance. The Sixth Connecticut to lead and attack the Southeast salient angle of the fort. The Forty-eighth New York to pass along the sea front and facing inward, to attack there; the other regiments of the brigade to charge the South front, extending inward towards the marshes, on the left; the Fifty-fourth Massachusetts Volunteers (colored), one thousand strong, in advance of all, and to be the "*enfans perdus.*" They formed in two lines ahead of the brigade. Their commander was Colonel Rob't G. Shaw. He was under the medium height, of a neat figure, wore a short jacket, and had long light hair, which fell low on his neck, nearly to his shoulders, giving him a very boyish appearance. Of the success of the assault there was no doubt. They thought that the guns of Wagner had all been silenced; that there were not five hundred

men in the fort, and these had been well hammered all day.
" We'll sleep in Wagner to-night," they said, and many a
poor fellow did, " the sleep that knows no waking."

SECOND ASSAULT, JULY 18TH.

By preconcerted arrangement, as night closed in, about a
quarter past 8 o'clock, all the Federal guns, land and sea,
ceased in a moment, and a great calm followed, a prelude
to a greater storm to burst anon in all its fury. As the
curtain of smoke, which like a pall had enveloped Wagner
all day, slowly lifted, the blue coats of the enemy were seen
debouching from their first parallel, and advancing over the
narrow approach between it and the fort. Quickly the garrison of Wagner sallied forth from the bomb-proof and sand
hills in the rear, to take their allotted positions on the ramparts, to do all that skill could dictate and manhood accomplish in defence of the place. The light field pieces were
dug out of the sand, remounted and placed in position, the
artillerists loaded their guns, double-shotted with grape and
canister, and stood lanyards in hand. Three companies of
the Charleston Battalion, under the intrepid Lieutenant-
Colonel P. C. Gaillard, manned the right of the battery;
next on their left stood the gallant Fifty-first North Carolina Volunteers, six hundred and eighty-seven strong, under
Colonel H. McKethan. The regiment that was to have
occupied the Southeast salient cowardly failed to respond,
and remained in the bomb-proof,* and thus was that portion of the battery undefended. The remaining two companies of the Charleston Battalion occupied the extreme
left of the fort by the beach.

When the advancing column was five hundred yards distant the blizzard burst; shot, shell, grape, shrapnel, canister and musket balls poured like hail and rain upon the
narrow approach, while Sumter, Gregg and the James Island

---

*This regiment wiped out the stigma incurred in a moment of weakness,
caused by the demoralizing effect of a new and strange experience, by their
distinguished bravery the next year in the operations around Petersburg.

batteries concentrated their shells rapidly and fatally on the same spot. For the morning bombardment the Federals were paid in their own coin.

Colonel Robert G. Shaw, with his colored troops, led the attack: "They went forward at a 'double quick' with great energy and resolution; but on approaching the ditch they broke; the greater part of them followed their intrepid Colonel, bounded over the ditch, mounted the parapet, and planted their flag in the most gallant manner upon the ramparts, where Shaw was shot dead; while the rest were siezed with a furious panic, and acted like wild beasts let loose from a menagerie. They came down first on the Ninth Maine, and then on the Seventy-sixth Pennsylvania, and broke both of them in two. Portions of the Ninth and Seventy-sixth mingled with the fugitives of the Fifty-fourth, and could not be brought to the fort. They ran away like deer, some crawling on their hands and knees."*

The Sixth Connecticut, Colonel John L. Chatfield, succeeded in passing through this deadly fire, and made a furious charge on the Southeast undefended salient, and took it. Here for three hours they were penned in, no support having dared to follow across the fatal stretch before the fort. To retreat was worse than the advance. While .the action was in progress Captain W. H. Ryan, with his company (Irish Volunteers, of Charleston Battalion), had endeavored to dislodge these men, and had met his death. Major David Ramsay was then ordered to take a detail from his command to recapture the salient. As he was advancing a shot from the bomb-proof struck him in the back, and he too fell. By this time the enemy was in full retreat, shattered and demoralized, and the conflict was virtually ended. A fire of grape and musketry swept the faces of the salient, to prevent the retreat of the Sixth Connecticut, who had found lodgment there, until the Thirty-first Georgia Regiment (who had reached the Island during the assault with Brigadier-General Hagood) charged over the Southern scarp, and two companies of the Charleston Battalion, under

*See "Life Afloat and Ashore," Judge Cowley, page 93.

Captain Julius A. Blake, of the Charleston Riflemen, deployed along the Western face, when the Sixth Connecticut surrendered. The assault was bravely made, but was doomed to failure from the onset. The demoralization of the negro troops at the supreme moment threw the ranks of the Federals into disorder. The converging fire of artillery and infantry on the narrow approach prevented a rally. Few could move within that fatal area and live. The situation of the work forbid any feint or diversion, so that the garrison could concentrate their attention on one point alone. Besides, the increasing darkness, rendered more dense by the smoke of conflict, added to the confusion of the assailants and helped the assailed, and thus the fortunes of war once more smiled on Fort Wagner, giving to the Confederates a complete victory and to the Federals an overwhelming defeat.

MAJOR DAVID RAMSAY.

One of the " bright, peculiar stars " of South Carolina was this scholar, statesman, soldier, gentleman. Unsurpassed in intellect, improved by ripe and faithful study in the Universities of Europe and America, he was fulfilling the promise of his early youth. Grandson of the great Henry Laurens, and also of South Carolina's historian, he had inherited the endowments of both grandsires, and to him the future was big with hope and promise. While gallantly leading his command he fell, not by the hand of the foe. For seventeen days he lingered, enduring his sufferings with Christian fortitude, and expired at last in his ancestral home. At heart a lover of the Union he fought to destroy, but a martyr to the State to which he deemed his allegiance was due.

LIEUTENANT-COLONEL JOHN C. SIMKINS.

No officer stood higher in personal worth, or was more beloved by his comrades and men than Lieutenant-Colonel Simkins, of the First South Carolina Infantry, and none have left behind them a brighter or purer memory. He fell in the front, cheering his brave artillerists, a noble type, living and dying, of a perfect gentleman and a brave soldier.

CAPTAIN WILLIAM H. RYAN.

Of all citizens, native or adopted, who have illustrated Irish zeal, devotion and courage in defence of South Carolina, no better or worthier name can be found than that of Captain Ryan, of the "Irish Volunteers." These names, Ramsay, Simkins, Tatum and Ryan, the martyrs of the 18th June, are inseparably connected with the defence of this renowned fort.

AFTER THE BATTLE.

Language has not the power to describe the horrors of the night succeeding that assault. The shattered columns of the Federals were driven back to the shelter of the sand hills. Four thousand men had been dashed against Fort Wagner ; when re-formed within the Federal lines only six hundred answered to their names. Brigadier-General Strong was mortally wounded, and Colonels Chatfield, Putnam and Shaw were left dead within the lines of the enemy. A desultory fire of small arms, with an occasional discharge of grape and canister, was kept up for a time at an unseen foe from the ramparts of Wagner. But soon silence and stillness reigned supreme, broken only now and then by the moans of the wounded and dying. At last the long night was ended, and the sun of a peaceful Sabbath rose, revealing the details of the sickening scene. " Blood, mud, water, brains and human hair, matted together ; men lying in every possible attitude, with every conceivable expression on their countenances ; their limbs bent into unnatural shapes by the fall of twenty or more feet ; the fingers rigid and out-stretched, as if they had clutched at the earth to save themselves ; pale, beseeching faces, looking out from among the ghastly corpses, with moans and cries for help and water, and dying gasps and death struggles." In the salient and on the ramparts they lay heaped and pent, in some places three deep. Among them Colonel Putnam, with the back part of his head blown off; still the remarkable beauty of his face and form evoked from his victorious foes a sigh of pity; while on the crest, with but few of his "sable troop" beside the flag he had vainly planted, was the youthful corpse of Colonel Shaw.

All of Sunday was employed in removing the wounded and burying the dead. The former were immediately taken to the city, and were carefully tended by Confederate Surgeons.* Wounds being inflicted at such short distance, little could be done save to amputate, and Federal blood flowed by the bucket full. Eight hundred mangled bodies, many of them shattered beyond recognition, so that 'twas hard to tell the black from the white, were buried by the Confederates before their fort, near the beach, to be unearthed again by the advancing sap and Federal shells. The wounded and dead more remote from Wagner were cared for by their friends.

EXCHANGE OF PRISONERS.

The next eventful day for Fort Wagner was the 25th of July. General Taliaferro had been relieved on the 19th by General Hagood, and was now again in command of the fort. The intervening time had been diligently employed by its defenders in repairing breaches, replacing guns, and otherwise strengthening the works. The Federals swarmed like bees nine hundred yards away on their second parallel, against which the enfilading batteries of James Island, and the guns of Wagner and Sumter, directed a continuous fire.

---

*Major Lewis Butler, of the Sixty-seventh Ohio, who was by the side of Colonel Putnam when the latter was killed, says: "It is but just that I notice a Special Order of General Beauregard, under date of July 27, 1863 (if I am correct as to date), directing that special care be taken of the wounded captured at Wagner, as men who were brave enough to go in there deserved the respect of their enemy. Another act of courtesy: the effects, money and papers belonging to members of the Sixty-seventh Ohio Volunteer Infantry, who died in Charleston Hospital, were sent through the lines by flag of truce."

Daily the monitors and New Ironsides threw into Wagner their 11 and 15-inch shells, and each night portions of its worn out garrison were relieved by fresh troops from Charleston.

Negotiations, through flags of truce, commencing just after the last assault, culminated in arrangements for an exchange of prisoners, the excess at this time being in the hands of the Confederates, and the 27th of July was appointed as the day. As the fleet had fired upon Wagner pending a flag of truce a few days before, for which an apology was demanded and given, Brigadier-General Ripley, commanding the district, ordered all his batteries not to fire on that day until after the exchange had been made. Not so the Federals. Early in the morning their whole iron-clad fleet took position abreast of this devoted fort ; and their earth-works, five hundred yards nearer than before, and mounted with still heavier guns, opened a concentrated and destructive fire, which, while it lasted, was equal in intensity to the bombardment of the 18th. Practice had made their aim more perfect, so that their shot sought out the weakest spots in the fort. The immense 15-inch shells of the monitors would roll slowly up the scarp and burst upon the crest of the work, some falling inside the gun chambers. The garrison sought shelter in the bomb-proof, or lay low behind the traverses and epaulments. All their guns were silent. The Island trembled as if from an earthquake.

At 10 o'clock the steamer conveying the Federal prisoners, with a large white flag at her fore, was seen passing Sumter. As she approached the fleet the bombardment ceased, and for four hours the negotiations were carried on by the two belligerent powers.

This time was diligently employed by General Taliaferro in the examination of the fort, which it was feared had been seriously damaged. The magazines and bomb-proofs were filled with smoke from exploding shells, leading to the belief that the former had been breached. So the garrison was set to work removing the powder from the Southeast magazine to one less exposed. No work or repairs could

4

be put upon the outside of the battery at this time, as to do
so would have betrayed to their vigilant foe the success of
their bombardment. All that could be done was to be on
the alert for another assault, which was expected.

PREPARATIONS FOR EVACUATION.

While the exchange of prisoners was going on, a
Council was called by General Taliaferro to discuss the
situation. It was decided that the place was no longer ten-
able, and must be given up. Dispatches were accordingly
signaled to General Ripley, asking that transportation be
furnished that night to remove the troops from the Island,
and preparation was made by General Taliaferro to evacu-
ate. But there was at least one officer in Fort Wagner who
did not share this feeling of insecurity. From the first
spadeful of sand thrown up he had seen the fort grow to
completion, and had assisted in and superintended the
work. He knew by personal inspection the depth of sand
remaining on the outside of the bomb-proofs and magazines
after the bombardment, and believed that, though their
form had changed, they were still practically intact. Asking and receiving permission to go to the city (with a reflection on the nature of the request at such a time), he manned
the gig of the Gist Guard Artillery, and proceeded at once
to the city and to General Ripley's headquarters. There he
found the General chafing over the situation, and after a
brief interview, in which he begged the General not to evac-
uate the Island, he was assigned to duty as Chief of
Artillery, and directed to return to Fort Wagner with
orders that it be held. The situation was also sub-
mitted to General Beauregard, and " instructions were sent
to General Taliaferro not to abandon the works without ex-
press orders to that effect."* So that incidentally through
the personal efforts of Captain C. E. Chichester, Wagner,
and indeed the city itself, was saved at that date from falling into the hands of the enemy; for the fall of Wagner then

*See General Ripley's report, p. 33, and General Beauregard, Vol. 2, p. 494.

would have gravely impaired the safety of Charleston, as the defences in the inner harbor were incomplete and defective.

END OF FIRST PERIOD.

Brigadier-General Johnson Hagood succeeded Brigadier-General Taliaferro in command of Morris Island on the night of 26th July, and thus ended the first sixteen days of the siege of Fort Wagner. Up to that time the following commands had performed duty on the Island, relieving each other at stated intervals, to wit: Artillery—Gist Guard, Lieutenant R. C. Gilchrist ; Matthewes Artillery, Captain J. Raven Matthews; Companies I, E and H, First South Carolina Artillery, Captains John C. Mitchell, J. R. Macbeth, and Lieutenant H. W. Frost; Captains Tatum and Adams' Companies, of the First South Carolina Infantry ; DeSaussure Light Artillery, Captain DePass commanding ; Captains Buckner and Dixon's Companies, of Sixty-third Georgia Regular Artillery ; Captains John H. Gary (Co. A) and Robert Pringle (Co. B), of Lucas' Battalion of Artillery. Infantry—Twenty-first Regiment South Carolina Volunteers, Colonel R. F. Graham ; Charleston Battalion, Lieutenant-Colonel P. C. Gaillard and Major David Ramsay; Company B, Captain Chas. T. Haskell, First South Carolina Infantry ; Twelfth and Eighteenth Georgia Battalions, under Lieutenant-Colonel H. D. Capers and Major W. S. Bassinger; Thirty-second Georgia Volunteers, Colonel Geo. P. Harrison ; Sixty-first North Carolina Volunteers, Colonel Jas. D. Radcliffe ; Fifty-first Regiment North Carolina Volunteers, Colonel Hector McKethan; Thirty-first North Carolina Volunteers, Lieutenant-Colonel Chas. W. Knight, and Eighth North Carolina Volunteers, Colonel Henry M. Shaw.

Out of these commands ninety-five had been killed, three hundred and twelve wounded and one hundred and thirty-two taken prisoners. Two desperate assaults had been repulsed, inflicting a loss on the Federals of not less than three thousand three hundred men. The guns disabled or dismounted in Fort Wagner had been renewed or replaced.

The effects of the heavy bombardment of the combined artillery of land and navy against an earth-work, unprecedented in the annals of war, on two occasions, aggregating twenty-one hours, and intermittent night and day, through the whole period, had been repaired by its garrison, working all of each and every night. General W. B. Taliaferro had succeeded Colonel Graham, was succeeded by General Johnson Hagood, succeeded him again, and was finally relieved of the command of the Island on the 26th July by General Hagood. From this time until the evacuation of the Island, Generals A. H. Colquitt and T. L. Clingman, and Colonels Geo. P. Harrison and L. M. Keitt, succeeded each other in command, serving generally about five days—General Hagood and Colonel Keitt having two tours of duty.

During this same period, notwithstanding their heavy losses, the Federals had accomplished substantial work. The 10th of July had given them three-fourths of Morris Island. On that day they established their first line, one thousand six hundred yards distant from Wagner. By gradual approaches, working night and day under a heavy fire from Sumter, Wagner, Gregg and the batteries on James Island, they had advanced eleven hundred yards, and were then one thousand yards distant from Wagner. Battery Reynolds, one thousand three hundred and thirty yards from Wagner, had been converted into a strong defensive line, capable of resisting a formidable sortie. A row of inclined palisading, reaching entirely across the Island, had been planted two hundred yards in advance of it, with a return of fifty yards on the right. A bomb-proof magazine was constructed, and heavy guns mounted. The first and second parallels were established and completed. The latter about six hundred yards in advance of the first, and occupying a narrow ridge which stretched across the Island and extended over the marsh to Vincent's Creek, which was spanned by two booms of floating timber to keep off sorties from boats. An obstacle consisting of abattis, inclined palisading and wire entanglements, was placed several yards in advance, flanked by six light guns. On the right the parallel itself was extended by a defensive barricade to low water mark, terminating at that point in a strong cut work, on which was placed three Riqua batteries and two field howitzers to sweep the beach. Thus were the opposing forces mutually prepared for attack and defence. General Gilmore at that time had double the available force of General Beauregard, within striking distance, and it would have been madness to attempt to drive him from the Island, protected as he was on the flank by the iron-clads.

SIEGE COMMENCES.

The unsuccessful assaults and bombardments of Wagner had impressed the Federal commander with a respect for its strength, and induced a change in his plan of operation. He abandoned all hope of taking it by "*coup de main*," and resolved to resort to the safer, but slower, method of siege by regular approach and bombardment. The large force at his disposal, aided by the fleet, which could protect his flank within the distance of a mile, rendered this practicable. His only difficulty, the shifting nature of the material he had to dig in, and the narrow ground on which to approach. But here, also, while his right flank was protected by the iron-clads, his left was equally so by an impassable marsh, and was only exposed to the fire of the batteries on James Island, two and a quarter miles distant.

At first Sumter seriously interfered with his work, delivering from its barbette guns, over Wagner, an accurate and destructive fire. But it was early eliminated from the conflict, those guns having been dismounted by the 18th of August by the breaching guns on Morris Island.

LIFE IN FORT WAGNER.

From the 20th of July was a period of simple endurance on Morris Island. Night and day, with scarcely any intermission, the hurling shell burst over and within it. Each

day, often from early dawn, the New Ironsides or the six
monitors, some times all together, steamed up and delivered
their terrific broadsides, shaking the fort to its centre.   The
noiseless coehorn shells, falling vertically, searched out the
secret recesses, almost invariably claiming victims.   The
burning sun of a Southern summer, its heat intensified by
the reflection of the white sand, scorched and blistered
the unprotected garrison, or the more welcome rain and
storm wet them to the skin.   An intolerable stench from
the unearthed dead of the previous conflict, the carcasses of
cavalry horses lying where they fell in the rear, and barrels
of putrid meat thrown out on the beach, sickened the defenders.   A large and brilliantly colored fly, attracted by
the feast, and unseen before, inflicted wounds more painful,
though less dangerous, than the shot of the enemy.   Water
was scarcer than whiskey.   The food, however good when
it started for its destination, by exposure, first on the
wharf in Charleston, then on the beach at Cummings Point,
being often forty-eight hours in transitu, was unfit to eat.
The unventilated bomb-proofs, filled with smoke of lamps
and smell of blood, were intolerable, so that one endured
the risk of shot and shell rather than seek its shelter.

The incessant din of its own artillery, as well as the
bursting shells of the foe, prevented sleep.   Then, as never
before, all realized the force of the prophecy: " In the
morning thou shalt say, would God it were even! and at
even thou shalt say, would God it were morning! for the
fear of thine eyes, wherewith thou shalt fear, and for the
sight of thine eyes which thou shalt see."

The casualties were not numerous, and yet each day
added to the list of killed and wounded.   Amputated
limbs were brought out from the hospital and buried in
the sand.   Often bodies followed them.   Only as a special
favor, or where high rank claimed the privilege, were the
dead carried to the city for interment.   There were few
in the battery who could not tell of some narrow escape,
where a movement of position only had saved life.   Nor can
we specify the instances of personal heroism, where all were

brave ; so often was the flag rescued and remounted, that orders were issued by the Commanding General forbidding it ; flags were many, but men were few. Thus the days lengthened into weeks, the weeks into months, while its brave and patient defenders individually stood face to face with death, and endured in many instances what was worse.

Nor was the garrison inactive. For the blows received, blows were given. Several monitors retired worsted from the encounter, and were not seen again. Explosions in the advancing works of the enemy showed the accuracy of the Confederate fire ; while every night through the weary hours lengthening into new days their working parties swarmed over the fort to repair the damage done to bomb-proof, parapet and traverses. Fighting from early morn to set of sun, and working through the livelong night, comprised their sum of life and daily experience.

It was not possible for human endurance to stand this mental and physical strain long. As each command became exhausted it was relieved, and fresh troops took their place. Six days was the longest period of any command ; the infantry served only three days at a time. And no greater proof can be had of their courage and devotion than that, with personal knowledge of the perilous nature of the service, the same commands returned time and again, with full ranks and even greater "*esprit de corps*," as the fierce struggle grew more intense.

As early as the 30th July the Federals secured the range of Cummings Point, on which they kept up a fire each night, and thus interrupted communication. Only occasionally after this could a steamer reach that landing, and then at great risk. One, the steamer " Sumter," was sunk by the batteries on Sullivan's Island, being mistaken for the enemy. So that by friend and foe alike, in the darkness of the night, was the relief of Morris Island endangered. Small boats alone, generally furnished by the Confederate Navy, supplied or changed the garrison in the last days of the siege, and these were harrassed, and sometimes captured, by the Federal barges that picketed nightly in the adjacent waters.

FEDERAL APPROACH.

By the 26th July the defensive arrangements of the second parallel were completed. They comprised, beside the formidable obstacles in front of it already described, two hundred and ninety yards of parapet for infantry and twenty-one pieces of light artillery, three 30-pounder Parrott rifles and one Wiard field gun—as strong against open assault as Wagner itself. Afterwards, by the 15th August, two 8-inch Parrott rifles and six 100-pounder Parrott rifles were located in this parallel against Fort Sumter, three thousand five hundred and twenty-five yards distant. At the same time the navy established in the first parallel two 200-pounder Parrott rifles and two 80-pounder Whitworth rifles, as a breaching battery. This was called "Naval Battery."

At "Battery Reynolds," on a line with Naval Battery, were mounted one 300-pounder Parrott rifle, two 200-pounder Parrott rifles and four 100-pounder Parrott rifles. All these pieces took part in the bombardment of Sumter from 17th to 23d August.

On August 9th the third parallel was established, with the flying sap about five hundred yards distant from Wagner, but their progress was greatly impeded, and on the 10th was stopped entirely by the Confederate batteries and the sharp-shooters, so that it became doubtful if the trenches could be pushed forward much further. Operations against Wagner were suspended until the 18th of August, and the attention of the Federals was directed chiefly against Sumter. The iron-clad fleet, however, from day to day continued to bombard both Wagner and Gregg.

From the 16th to the 24th of August, the fourteen 100, 200 and 300-pounder Parrott rifle breaching guns of the Federal batteries were directed almost exclusively on Fort Sumter, firing five thousand and nine projectiles weighing five hundred and fifty-two thousand six hundred and eighty-three pounds, though seriously interfered with, and at times partially suspended, by the galling fire from Fort Wagner. The combined fire of their mortars and light pieces, aided by the gun boats and iron-clads, failed to subdue this annoyance, so the Federals turned some of their heavy breaching guns on that work. At one time there was a prospect that their most efficient batteries would be disabled before they had accomplished their work of demolition of Sumter.

On the night of August 18th active operations were resumed against Wagner, by debouching with the full sap from the left of the third parallel. The high tides and storm, usual at this season, had submerged the trenches to a depth of two feet in many places and washed down the parapets. At the second parallel the "Surf Battery" had barely escaped destruction, about one-third of it having been carried away to the sea. Its armament had been temporarily removed as a precaution against the storm. The progress of the sap being hotly opposed by the fire of both artillery and sharp-shooters in Wagner, and by the latter, in particular, under the cover of the ridge, two hundred yards in front of the battery.

On the 21st August the fourth parallel was opened three hundred yards distant from Fort Wagner, partly with the flying and partly with the full sap. Here the Island is one hundred and sixty yards wide at high water.

ARTILLERY PRACTICE.

The constant service of the guns on both sides made the artillerists almost perfect in their aim. The Federals, having better guns and ammunition, were the most accurate. From a land battery an 8-inch rifle shot was fired at a siege howitzer on the land face of Wagner. It struck the muzzle. The Captain of the squad said it was a chance shot, and told his men to run her "in battery" again. The next shot came swiftly, and entering the bore broke the piece off at the trunnions. The 11 and 15-inch shells from the Ironsides and monitors fired at a low elevation would richochet, or rather roll, on the water, and striking the edge of the beach bound over the parapet, to burst in a gun chamber or passage-way. One such shell claimed as its victim the

engineer in charge, Captain Wampler, who had arrived at
Wagner only a short time before. He had just taken the
chair vacated by Surgeon Henry B. Horlbeck, and seating
himself to write, had commenced "My dear wife and
child," when the deafening report of the shell was
heard and he was seen to slide from his chair cut in
twain. He died without a moan. The excellence of their
fuses made their mortar practice superb. Seldom did they
fail to burst either just over or within the fort.

If the fire of the Confederate batteries was less effective,
it must be remembered that the largest gun was a 10-inch
Columbiad, never in prime condition and things always
awry. The gunners, also, instead of being within a turret
of iron or beyond range of adverse fire, were terribly exposed; yet, of the accuracy of their aim let Admiral Dahlgren speak. He says: "On August 17 the Ironsides lay at
nine hundred yards, and was struck thirty-one times, mostly
from Wagner and Gregg." "During the operations against
Morris Island the nine iron-clads fired eight thousand and
twenty-six projectiles, weighing six hundred and fifty-three
and a half tons, and were hit eight hundred and eighty-two
times, chiefly by 10-inch shot." "The duties of the iron-
clads were not performed under idle batteries; the guns of
Wagner never failed to open on them, and fired until their
men were driven by those of our iron-clads to take shelter
in the bomb-proofs. One of their cannon, a 10-inch, left
deep dents on every turret that will not easily be effaced."
Had that gun been a 300-pounder rifled Parrott, or one of
the 9¼-inch 700-pounder rifled Blakely afterwards mounted
in Charleston, its record would have been fatal to every
iron-clad.

SHARP-SHOOTERS.

More fatal even than the heaviest artillery were the little
minnie balls of the sharp-shooters. "From early morn to
dewy eve," these crack shots would sit in their eyries, ex-
temporized out of sand bags, patiently watching for a mark

to fire at. To expose a hat, an arm or a hand even on either side was sure to draw a minnie ball with certain aim from over one thousand yards away. A cap elevated on a ram-rod above the parapet would draw the fire of the foe, and when the incautious "blue jacket" peered out of his rifle pit to see the effect of his shot he was "plugged." An officer in Wagner making his rounds looked for a moment through one of these loop-holes at the advancing sap, a puff of smoke from a rifle pit warned him of his danger and he withdrew his head just in time to escape the ball that passed through the opening. Another less fortunate was pierced through his brain. This accuracy of aim was due to the Whitworth rifle, with telescopic attachment, ob-tained for Wagner through the efforts of Capt. S. A. Ashe, of the Ordnance Department, who did good service on Mor-ris Island during the greater part of the siege. These guns were fatal at fifteen hundred yards. The heavy charge at which they were fired caused a recoil that bruised the face of the sharp-shooter, so that the black ring around the eye was recognized as his distinctive badge.

CAVALRY.

Strange as it may seem, the cavalry rendered efficient service on Morris Island. A detail of a Lieutenant and ten men, with their horses, from Capt. Zimmerman Davis' com-pany, "The South Carolina Rangers," were sent down on the 11th July, and thereafter until the evacuation reliefs were furnished by the same command; the same horses being used by each. The duty these men performed was dangerous in the extreme. They were the couriers between Fort Wagner and Battery Gregg, and as one started at full speed from one to the other he became at once a target for the shells from the monitors and balls from the sharp-shooters, and it was always a race for life. Many narrow escapes were made. Privates Flinn C. Davis and W. W. Pemberton had their horses killed under them. Frequently an important dispatch would be sent by two

36 *Confederate Defence of Morris Island.*

couriers at a time, so as to ensure its delivery should one be killed. In the assault of the 18th July, Lieut. Geo. Tupper with his squad and the relief under Lieut. J. P. DeVeaux, Jr., (making twenty men) were present, and while not acting as couriers, rendered valuable aid in repelling the assault, engaging in a hand-to-hand conflict with the enemy.

THE SIGNAL CORPS.

Though non-combatants, none ran greater risks than the signal corps. Perched on the highest and most conspicuous spot of Battery Gregg, flag in hand—the cynosure of all eyes, both friend and foe, exposed to the fire of sharp-shooter and artillery, often their special aim, in the thick as well as the surcease of conflict—the wig-wag of their flags conveyed to the commandant in Charleston the needs of the garrison, or received from him orders for defence. By their intelligent service, likewise, the dispatches passing from fleet to shore were read; so that, forewarned by them on several occasions, the Confederates were forearmed and ready, so as to repel with little loss assaults that would otherwise have been fatal.

SURGEONS AND CHAPLAINS.

Without the excitement of conflict to lessen the sense of danger, in the midst of scenes that "tried men's souls," and exposed to risks as imminent and great as the actual combatants endured, the Surgeon and the Chaplain in Wagner had to perform the demands of their calling, sustained only by a sense of duty. In the intolerable heat and stench of the bomb-proof, suffocated with the smoke of lamp oil that could find no vent, in darkness relieved at noon-day by its fitful glare, the Surgeon staunched the life-blood and bound up the gaping wounds of his comrades, or sought to save life by the sacrifice of limbs; while the devoted Chaplain, with heartfelt pity and gentle smile, kneeled by the side of the wounded to whisper the peace and consolation Heaven alone could give. Notably among these heroic Chaplains was the Rev. Samuel E. Axson, who always accompanied his comrades to the rifle pits, sharing their danger, animating them by precept and example in the supreme moment of conflict, receiving from the dying the last message of love to absent dear ones, and, as far as human sympathy could avail, sustaining them as they passed through " the valley of the shadow of death."

ASSAULT ON RIFLE PITS.

The ridge two hundred and forty yards in front of Fort Wagner was the source of serious annoyance to the approaching sap of the Federals. It was occupied by the Confederate sharp-shooters, who kept up a deadly fire on their gunners and working party. Brigadier-General Terry was ordered to " carry it at the point of the bayonet and hold it." As preliminary to the assault the monitors shelled it and Wagner heavily during the day of the 21st, firing sixty shots to the minute, and about dark the attempt was made. They were received with a brisk fire and a determined front, and reinforcements being sent forward by General Hagood, the assault was driven back. Among the killed on that day was Captain Robert Pringle, of Lucas' Battalion of Artillery, who had served with distinction on Coles' Island, and was then acting as Chief of Artillery. That morning, while the monitors were shelling Wagner vigorously, their shells fired at low elevation would ricochet twice upon the water, the last time about twenty-five yards from the shore, and then explode just over the parapet of the battery. One of these shells struck a school of mullet, and hurled one into the gun-chamber. Captain Pringle picked it up, and laughingly remarked, " I have got my dinner." Not long after he was killed.

FIRST ASSAULT ON GREGG.

On the 24th of August an attempt was made to carry Cummings Point from Vincent's Creek. Lieutenant R. C.

Gilchrist was then in command of Battery Gregg, with the Gist Guard Artillery and Company C of Lucas' Battalion of Artillery as its garrison. By some means the Federal signal code had been obtained, so that messages passing between the fleet and shore could be read.* By this means the Confederates were informed of the contemplated attack that night; further confirmed by the vigorous shelling of Battery Gregg all that day, during which a heavy traverse caved in, filling up the gun-chamber, burying the gunners of Company C, Lucas' Battalion. A volunteer party, headed by Sergeant Brown, of the Marion Artillery, flew to the rescue of their comrades and dug them out, while exposed to a concentrated fire of artillery and sharp-shooters, but not before two were dead. The guns of Battery Gregg were trained to sweep the creek just beyond the shore. A select picket force was stationed to watch for the approach of the barges. About midnight the phosphorescent light made by the splash of muffled oars alone revealed their presence. The signal was given; grape, canister and lead responded; while the crash of timbers and shrieks of the wounded told of the efficacy of the aim. In five minutes the conflict was ended.

CAPTURE OF RIDGE.

The unsuccessful assault on the rifle-pits of the 21st was renewed on the 25th August. As long as this post could be held it was not possible to surprise Wagner, so it was the "*point d' appui*" for both assailed and assailant. General Hagood's forces were fortunately prepared to receive the attack, and the position was held with courage and spirit by the Sixty-first North Carolina and the Fifty-fourth Georgia Regiments, by whom the enemy was driven back a second time, with heavy loss, the casualties on the Confederate side being but five killed and nineteen wounded.

* On board the monitor "Keokuk" a copy of the Federal signal code was found. Armed with this, one of the Confederate Signal Corps, dressed in a "blue jacket," was locked up as a fellow-prisoner with one of the Federal Signal Corps; from him he learned it perfectly.

The following day Fort Wagner was subjected to another of those heavy bombardments from land and sea to which it had become accustomed, and at dark an overwhelming force was thrown against the " Ridge." The engagement of the night before had interrupted communication with the city, so that reinforcements of fresh troops and ammunition failed to reach the Island. Overpowered at last, the ridge was abandoned, and the fifth and last parallel against Wagner established.

BEGINNING OF THE END.

The massive walls of Fort Sumter had been battered down until they were a shapeless ruin. Its gallant artillery defenders could do little more than lie passive. The heavy armament, which had done good service on the 7th of April, had been removed, and was then guarding the inner defences of Charleston. The long and stubborn defence of Fort Wagner had served its purpose. *The demolition of Sumter did not open the gate to the city.* Frowning batteries lined the inner harbor, prepared to meet with shot and shell, hurled by the same brave hands, the armored fleet of the foe. Still, as before the destruction of Sumter, the enemy did not dare to essay an entrance into the harbor. The commander of the fleet, as if with premonition of the fate that would befall him, utterly failed to realize the expectations which had been based upon the supposed efficiency of the iron-clads. The time had therefore come when Wagner had ceased to be useful, and there was no longer a call for sacrifice of life in its defence.

The Federals were now two hundred and fifty yards from the sally port of Fort Wagner. The intervening space comprised the narrowest and shallowest part of Morris Island, over which the sea in rough weather swept entirely across. It had been the intention of Captain Cheves to cut through this portion, making a canal, which would have widened with each recurring tide, thus dividing the Island at that point. Had this been done no sap could have approached nearer.

An ingenious system of torpedo mines, to be exploded by the tread of persons walking over them, had been established by the Confederates in this narrow causeway and in front of the battery. These protected the enemy against sorties even more than they impeded his approach.

The Federals were now so near to Wagner that they were comparatively free from the enfilading fire of the James Island batteries, and were exposed only to the converging fire of Wagner and its sharp-shooters. The bright moon impeded work by night almost as well as the sun by day, and the casualties of the sappers were on the increase. It was therefore determined to keep Wagner quiet with an overpowering curved fire from siege and coehorn mortars, and if possible to breach the bomb-proof shelter with rifled guns. Accordingly, all the light mortars were moved to the front and placed in battery; the rifled guns were trained upon Wagner and prepared for prolonged action; a large magazine was constructed to furnish ample supplies of ammunition, and the co-operation of the New Ironsides during the day was secured.

LAST BOMBARDMENT.

At break of day on the morning of the 5th of September seventeen siege and coehorn mortars, thirteen 100, 200 and 300-pounder Parrott rifles, opened on the devoted battery, which still loomed up as defiantly as ever. The New Ironsides took position a mile distant, and from her eight gun broadside poured an incessant blizzard of 11-inch shells against the sloping parapet, exploding either over or within the work. For forty-two consecutive hours this iron hail descended, making a scene as unsurpassingly grand as it was fearful. One thousand four hundred and eleven projectiles were thrown by the land batteries alone, aggregating 150,505 pounds of metal, 22,330 pounds striking the bomb-proof, and during the night, when the fire of the mortars was most needed, as many as four shells could be seen at once *en route* for Wagner. The garrison sought the shelter of bomb-proof, traverse and revetment, and the guns were silent. Powerful calcium lights turned night into day, blinding the defenders, giving light to the sappers, and enabling the Federal artillerists to fire with the same precision as in the day. No one could move within the range of those guns and live. The casualties on that day were one in nine.

During this bombardment the Federals in the advanced trenches prosecuted their labors without danger, pushing by the South face of the fort, leaving it on their left. By night they had advanced to the moat.

Fort Wagner had now been held under a continued and furious cannonade, by land and sea, night and day, for fifty-seven days. The Federals had been forced to expend time, men and material most lavishly in approaching it ; foot by foot burrowing their way with pick and shovel, they were at last within the moat. Nearly all the guns in the fort were injured and useless. Transportation of men and supplies had become most difficult and dangerous. The enemy were over eleven thousand five hundred strong on the Island, supported by a powerful fleet of iron-clads and gunboats, free to select their own time and method of attack. The calcium lights, placed on monitors at a safe distance abreast the fort, illuminated the works as brilliantly at night as the sun by day ; while their sharp-shooters, under shelter of the darkness, sent death to every one who was exposed, so that no repairs could be put upon the fort.

General Beauregard, who had for some time been considering the exigencies of the case, sent his Chief Engineer, Colonel Harris, with the Engineer of the post, Captain F. D. Lee, on Sunday, the 10th September, to make a critical examination of the fort, its capabilities of continued defence, and the position of the enemy's sap. On receiving his report, to save the brave men forming its garrison from the desperate chances of an assault, he gave orders for its evacuation.

BOAT ATTACK ON CUMMINGS POINT.

During the occupation of Morris Island by the Federals,

Battery Gregg, on Cummings Point, had played a part second only to Fort Wagner. Each day its garrison had come in for a share of the shelling, both from the fleet and land batteries, and full well had it discharged its duty in resisting the advance of the foe. On the night preceding the evacuation it occupied the foremost point of attack. On Saturday evening there were indications observed of an assault by boats. Colonel Keitt, now in command of the Island, sent strong reinforcements from the Twenty-eighth Georgia and Twenty-fifth South Carolina Volunteers to the support of Battery Gregg, who stationed themselves in the sand hills between it and Wagner. While taking their position, Captain Haines, of the Twenty-eighth Georgia, and Lieut. R. A. Blum, commanding Company B, Washington Light Infantry, Twenty-fifth South Carolina Volunteers, were both killed by a mortar shell. Two monitors were at that time shelling Gregg. At a quarter to 2 A. M. a rocket was thrown up, and ere many minutes elapsed the Federals were descried approaching Morris Island at a point between Wagner and Gregg, in fifteen or twenty barges, through the creek to the rear. Advancing in line of battle, they were permitted to come very near. Captain Henry R. Lesesne, commanding Gregg, opened on them with a 9-inch Dahlgren, with double canister and grape. Major Gardner, of the Twenty-seventh Georgia Regiment, threw his infantry forward and poured into them a well directed and effective fire of musketry. Moultrie, Batteries Bee and Mitchell also opened a rapid and most demoralizing fire. The barges pressed bravely forward, firing spherical case from their howitzers. Captain J. R. Macbeth (son of the Mayor of Charleston) replied with his two field howitzers. The Federals were soon compelled to withdraw, baffled once again in their attempt to capture Gregg, and thus take Wagner in the rear. As all who were struck fell in their boats, the loss was not known. Some bodies and debris of boats floated to the shore. The survivors made the best of their way back through the creek and marshes.

PREPARATIONS FOR EVACUATION.

The Confederate iron-clads took position just after dark on the evening of the 6th, near to Fort Sumter, with their guns bearing on Cummings Point to the Eastward of Gregg. At the same time all the James Island batteries were prepared to sweep the water faces of Gregg. Transport steamers took position within the harbor, near to Cummings Point, to receive the men from the row boats, by which the embarkation from Morris Island was to be effected. Forty barges, manned by proficient oarsmen from the " Palmetto State " and " Chicora," each under charge of a navy officer, the whole commanded by Lieutenant Ward, Confederate States Navy, were in readiness at Cummings Point at dark. On Morris Island, Colonel Keitt in command, made all necessary arrangements, assisted by Lieutenant-Colonel J. G. Pressley, Twenty-fifth South Carolina Volunteers (Eutaw Regiment); Major Gardner, Twenty-seventh Georgia Regiment; Captain W. P. Crawford, Twenty-eighth Georgia Regiment, and Captain T. A. Huguenin, First South Carolina Infantry.

The whole day the terrific bombardment had continued, adding to the casualties two-fold ; men fell on every side, and the litter-bearers and surgeons had their hands full. Yet in that solemn hour, in the gloom of the bomb-proof, the Rev. Andrew Flinn Dickson, the brave and devoted Chaplain of the Twenty-fifth Regiment, conducted the usual Sabbath services. Those gathered there were neither afraid nor ashamed to pray, and their deep toned voices ascended in the sweet songs of praise to the sad accompaniment of the groans of the wounded, and the sighs of the dying, while around and above them the shriek of balls and bursting of shells added to the earnestness of worship. A fit ending to that memorable siege.

On the approach of night Companies C and E, of the Twenty-fifth Regiment, were ordered to march in from the sand hills. This movement, no doubt, created the impression that the garrison was being changed, and that fresh

troops were coming in to relieve those on duty. When
night closed in Company E, Palmetto Battalion, Light
Artillery, Captain J. D. Johnson, and the Twenty-eighth
Georgia, moved out of the fort, and took position in the
sand hills, between it and Gregg, where the Twenty-seventh
Georgia had a 12-pounder howitzer, so as to check pursuit
long enough to enable every one to escape. At the same
time the wounded were sent back to Cummings Point. Company I, Twenty-fifth South Carolina Volunteers, Captain
Joseph C. Burgess, spread out over the land face of Wagner,
covering the space that had been occupied by the Twenty-
eighth Georgia, and kept up a steady fire, so as to induce
the belief that the fort had been reinforced.

General Gilmore, in command of the Federal forces, on
that day issued orders to assault Fort Wagner on the mor-
row, at 9 A. M., that being the hour of low tide, by the
troops in command of Brigadier-General Terry, detailing the
manner of the assault ; and the troops were so disposed in
the trenches that night.

THE EVACUATION.

There is no operation in war more delicate than the evacuation by water of a detached and remote fort, in the near
presence of the enemy. The Federals were in large force,
the head of their column in the sap, which had reached the
moat. Coolness, resolute courage, judgment and inflexi-
bility on the part of officers, obedience to orders, perfect
discipline, and a constant sense of the necessity for silence
on the part of the men, were essential for success. One de-
serter to the enemy would have defeated it. How easy in
the darkness and confusion of that night to slip around the
curtain to the sap, just a few steps beyond, and with one
word put in motion eleven thousand five hundred Federals.
That no traitor was there redounds to the eternal credit of
the garrison, and crowns the record that makes immortal
the fame of Fort Wagner.

There was a suspicion in the Federal mind that some

movement was taking place among the Confederates, but whether it was an increase of garrison, or an evacuation, no one could determine. To be prepared for any emergency, a strong calcium light was thrown upon the fort from one of the iron-clads. It was a ghostly glare, which betrayed those who watched, instead of those who retreated. Men moved about the works without discovery, and the light on the front of the fort deepened the darkness on all other sides, throwing the shadow of Wagner back over the sand hills all the way to Cummings Point.

At 9 o'clock Sunday night a courier informed Colonel Keitt that the boats were at the point in readiness for the embarkation. The wounded were first sent off. About this time First Sergeant Carson, of Company F, Twenty-fifth South Carolina Volunteers, was killed, and Lieutenant J. N. McDonald, commanding Company K, Twenty-fifth South Carolina Volunteers, mortally wounded. The former was buried by his comrades behind the flank wall of Wagner, the booming of the enemy's guns and the bursting of their shells his funeral salute. To the admirable discipline of the crews of the barges is mainly due the success of the embarkation. Their boats kept abreast, with the length of an oar from the gunwale to the end of the blade separating them. The oars thus interlocked never touched or interfered with each other. As each detachment left, other boats grounded on the beach to receive their load, and thus silently and without confusion the embarkation was accomplished.

To the Twenty-fifth Regiment South Carolina Volunteers was accorded the honor of bringing up the rear and guarding the retreat from the fort. As courier after courier arrived from Cummings Point, with information that the previous detachment had embarked, Lieutenant-Colonel Pressley sent off other companies, distributing those remaining over the works to keep up the firing. At last only he, with Companies I and F, remained. The soft sand echoed no foot-step, and no voice was raised above a whisper. Even to have spiked the cannon in Wagner would have notified the Federals in their sap, not thirty steps away, and so the armament was left intact. At midnight the fort, which had been tenanted so long, and had withstood so much, was without a sentinel to challenge or an artillerist to fire. Captain Huguenin, with Captain C. C. Pinckney, of General Ripley's Staff, Captain Edmund Mazyck, Ordnance Officer at Wagner, Captain Harry Bryan, of General Beauregard's Staff, assigned to duty with Colonel Keitt, and Lieutenant James Ross, of the Washington Light Infantry, and thirty-five men, selected from the different commands, were left behind as a rear guard, and to blow up the fort.

At Battery Gregg Captain C. E. Kanapaux, commanding the Light Artillery, spiked his guns and embarked his company. Captain Henry R. Lesesne, in command of Gregg, spiked the guns of that battery, and sent off his command, Company H, First South Carolina Artillery; and Colonel L. M. Keitt, with the remainder of the garrison, safely and expeditiously embarked about an hour after midnight, just as the moon was rising. The signal having been given, the fuses were lighted—that at Wagner by Capt. Huguenin and that at Gregg by Capt. Lesesne. Every precaution had been taken to ensure their efficiency, and they were so timed that the parties retreating from Wagner could embark with those from Gregg, and the destruction of the two fortifications occur simultaneously. Capt. Huguenin and party remained in Wagner longer than was prudent so as to be certain the fuse was burning, and did not leave until they had every assurance of success. Capt. Lesesne at Gregg, finding that his fuse was burning more rapidly than calculated, re-entered the magazine and cut off the lighted end, so as to give time for the arrival of the rear guard from Wagner, and when they were seen approaching he re-lit it. The whole party (except Capt. Huguenin, who had fallen to the rear on account of a wound in his knee), then embarked in the boat commanded by Lieut. Odenheimer (son of the Bishop of New Jersey), of the Confederate States Navy. About this time the Federal barges were swarming around

Cummings Point, and commanded the adjacent waters. Two boats, containing nineteen sailors and twenty-seven soldiers of the rear guard, had already been captured ; so Lieut. Odenheimer boldly put out to sea under fire of the boat howitzers. As they skirted the beach, to the surprise of all they were hailed by Capt. Huguenin, who waded out to his arm-pits and was drawn into the boat.

SURPRISE OF FEDERALS.

"No one at Home!" was the reply received the next morning when Gen. Gilmore knocked at the sally-port for admission. The elaborate preparation for an assault was useless. The Federals walked in quietly and took posses-sion. The brief official report of its "capture" (?) hardly conceals the chagrin felt at the "escape" of the "once de-fiant foe." The fuses which should have given warning of evacuated works, like most Confederate fuses, failed to do duty. The guns (hereafter enumerated) fell into the hands of the Federals, but to them they were only so much old iron, or trophies of war. Nevertheless, to signalize their barren victory they replaced with the "Stars and Stripes" the little battle flags floating over Wagner and Gregg.

SUMMARY.

For fifty-eight days Wagner and Gregg, with a force never exceeding sixteen hundred men, had withstood a thoroughly equipped army of eleven thousand five hundred men, the Ironsides, eight monitors and five gunboats. For every pound of sand used in construction or repair of Fort Wagner, its assailants had expended two pounds of iron in the vain attempt to batter it down. At the end of the bombardment, as at the commencement, it stood sullen, strong and defiant as ever. The total loss in killed and wounded on Morris Island from July 10th to September 7th, was only six hundred and seventy-two men. Deduct-ing the killed and wounded due to the landing on the 10th July and to the assaults of the 11th and 18th July, the

killed and wounded by the terrible bombardment which
lasted almost uninterruptedly night and day for fifty days,
only amounted to forty-seven killed and two hundred and
eighty men wounded, many of whom were but slightly
injured.

The days and weeks, lengthening into months, during
which the gallant defence was prolonged, had been employed by Gen. Ripley in erecting batteries along the shores
of the inner harbor, and in the city itself, in which were
mounted the heavy guns taken from Fort Sumter. The
debris of that grim old fortress, with other material brought
by night from the city under the orders of the Engineer
Department, and the engineer in charge (being for the most
part Major John Johnson, C. S. Engineer Corps, now the
Rector of St. Philip's Church, Charleston), had gradually
converted it into a powerful earth-work for infantry; its
brave artillery garrison having been removed to the interior
and still stronger line of batteries.

What, then, had the Federals gained by the lavish expenditure of the material of war, boundless treasure, and
the fearful sacrifice of life they had sustained during those
two weary months? The sole object of the occupation of
Morris Island, as stated by General Gilmore, was "the
demolition of Sumter as preliminary to the entrance of
the iron-clads." That accomplished, it was thought that
the gate to Charleston would be thrown open to the navy,
and the "Cradle of Secession" would fall. From the 30th of
August, 1863, only a morning and evening gun (32-pounder)
saluted its flag. Sumter was eliminated from the defence
of the harbor. Yet for eighteen months thereafter the fleet
remained in the outer harbor, viewing the spires of Charleston over the low hills of Morris Island, and all this time the
200 and 300-pounder rifle Parrotts mounted at Cummings
Point kept up ever and anon an ineffectual fire at St.
Michael's steeple and other points in the city. It was not
until the 18th of February, 1865, when a row boat, sent by
the Municipal authorities of Charleston, informed Admiral
Dahlgren in the outer harbor that the Confederate forces

had evacuated the city, and that the frowning batteries lining the shores of the Ashley and Cooper Rivers were without men to man their guns, did his fleet venture to enter; then, without fear of torpedo or harbor obstruction, did monitors and gunboats steam up to the wharves of the city.

Greek and Roman in ancient history, the English, French and German in modern, have their stories of heroic endurance, steadfast purpose and uncomplaining sacrifice, even unto death, but never did Greek, Spartan, Gaul, Teuton nor Anglo-Saxon show greater pluck and determination than were exhibited by the gallant defenders of Fort Wagner and Battery Gregg on Morris Island.

Federal history calls the capture of Wagner a great victory. *Victory! Seven hundred and forty men driven out of a sand hill by eleven thousand five hundred.* Two months to advance half a mile towards Charleston. They make their boast that Sumter was demolished over Wagner. This only teaches the world that sand batteries are more impregnable than the most solid masonry, especially when MEN are behind them who know how to fight them by day and repair them by night.

To-day that famed fort is leveled; its bomb-proofs, parapets and traverses blotted out; not by the iron hail of hostile batteries, but by the winds of heaven. What the wrath of man could not accomplish, the "still small voice" of the Almighty has done.

"Afflavit Deus et dissipantur."

Ere long the sea, with its white capped waves, will sweep athwart this page of our country's history, which has been written in blood—even the site of Fort Wagner will be gone. Not so its name and fame. Sooner will Thermopylæ, Marathon, Salamis, Sebastopol, and the other places where in the past men have dared, endured and died, be lost to memory, than will be forgotten the heroic patience and devoted courage of the soldiers who manned the defences of Morris Island.

7

OFFICERS IN COMMAND ON MORRIS ISLAND.

Brigadier-Generals Wm. Taliaferro, Johnson Hagood, T. L. Clingman, and A. H. Colquitt ; Colonels Geo. P. Harrison, Jr. and L. M. Keitt.

CHIEFS OF ARTILLERY.

Lieutenant-Colonels Jos. A. Yates, John C. Simkins, Del Kemper, J. Welsman Brown ; Major F. F. Warley, and Captains C. E. Chichester, T. A. Huguenin and Robert Pringle.*

ARTILLERY.

GIST GUARD ARTILLERY—Lieutenant R. C. Gilchrist.
MATTHEWES ARTILLERY—Captain J. Raven Matthewes.
FIRST SOUTH CAROLINA ARTILLERY—
       Company C—Captain C. W. Parker.
       Company E—Captain J. R. Macbeth.
       Company H—Captain H. R. Lesesne.
       Company K—Captain Alfred S. Gaillard.
       Company I—Captain John C. Mitchell.
SECOND SOUTH CAROLINA ARTILLERY—
       Company A—Lieutenant Robert S. Millar.
       Company F—Captain Thos. K. Legare.
FIRST SOUTH CAROLINA INFANTRY, AS ARTILLERY—
     . Company A—Captain T. A. Huguenin.
       Company B—Captain W. H. Tatem.*
       Company D—Captain Charles T. Haskell.
       Company H—Captain Warren Adams.
LUCAS' BATTALION ARTILLERY—
       Company A—Captain John H. Gary.
       Company B—Captain Robt. Pringle.*
       Company C—Captain T. B. Hayne.
PALMETTO BATTALION ARTILLERY—
       Company E—Captain J. D. Johnson.
       Company G—Captain W. L. DePass.
SOUTH CAROLINA SIEGE TRAIN—Company B, Lieutenant Ralph Nesbit.
TWELFTH BATTALION GEORGIA ARTILLERY—Company A, Captain G. N. Hanvey.
SIXTY-THIRD REGIMENT GEORGIA ARTILLERY—
       Company B—Captain James T. Buckner.
       Company K—Captain W. J. Dixon.
MARION ARTILLERY—Captain Edward L. Parker, Lieutenants John P. Strohecker, Robert S. Murdoch, Martin L. Wilkins and Henry D. Lowndes.
CHATHAM ARTILLERY—Lieutenants S. B. Palmer and T. A. Askew.
BLAKE ARTILLERY—Lieutenant T. D. Waties.

---

* Killed in Wagner.

CAVALRY (AS COURIERS).

SOUTH CAROLINA RANGERS—(Captain Zimmerman Davis) Lieutenants Geo. Tupper, J. P. DeVeaux, Jr., Geo. H. Smith.

INFANTRY.

SEVENTH SOUTH CAROLINA BATTALION—Lieutenant-Colonel Patrick H. Nelson.

TWENTIETH SOUTH CAROLINA VOLUNTEERS—(Colonel Keitt) Lieutenant-Colonel Olen Dantzler and Major E. Boykin.

TWENTY-FIRST SOUTH CAROLINA VOLUNTEERS—Colonel R. F. Graham, Lieutenant-Colonel Dargan and Major G. W. McIver.

Company A—Captain J. H. Read.
Company B—Captain S. H. Wilds.
Company D—Captain M. H. Tarrh.
Company E—Captain B. F. Davis.
Company F—Captain J. A. W. Thomas.
Company G—Captain R. W. Reddy.
Company H—Lieutenant J. H. Dalrymple.
Company I—Captain R. G. Howard.
Company K—Captain J. W. Owens.
Company L—Captain H. Legette.

TWENTY-FIFTH SOUTH CAROLINA VOLUNTEERS—(Colonel C. H. Simonton in command of James Island) Lieutenant Colonel J. G. Pressley and Major John V. Glover.

Company A (Washington Light Infantry)—Lieutenant H. B. Olney.*
Company B (Washington Light Infantry)—Lieutenant R. A. Blum.†
Company C (Wee Nee Volunteers)—Captain T. J. China.
Company D (Marion Light Infantry)—Captain W. J. McKerrall.
Company E (Beauregard Light Infantry)—Lieutenant A. J. Mims.
Company F (St. Matthewes Rifles)—Captain M. H. Sellers.
Company G (Edisto Rifles)—Captain J. F. Izlar.
Company H (Yeadon Light Infantry)—Captain Leroy F. Hammond.
Company I (Clarendon Rifles)—Captain Jos. C. Burgess.
Company K (Ripley Guards)—Captain W. B. Gordon.

CHARLESTON BATTALION—Lieutenant-Colonel P. C. Gaillard,‡ Major David Ramsay.§

Company A (Calhoun Guards)—Captain F. T. Miles.
Company B (Charleston Light Infantry) Captain Thos. Y. Simons.
Company C (Union Light Infantry and German Fusiliers)—Captain S. Lord, Jr.
Company D (Sumter Guards)—Captain J. Ward Hopkins.
Company E (Irish Volunteers)—Captain W. H. Ryan.‖
Company F (Charleston Riflemen)—Captain Julius A. Blake.

EIGHTH NORTH CAROLINA VOLUNTEERS—Colonel Henry M. Shaw, Lieu-
tenant-Colonel James M. Whitson, Major John R. Murchison.
  Company A—Captain Daniel A. Sawyer.
  Company B—Captain Thomas J. Jarvis.
  Company C—Captain Charles A. Barron.
  Company D—Captain Andrew J. Rogers.
  Company E—Captain Luther R. Breese.
  Company F—Captain Leonard A. Henderson.
  Company G—Captain Amos J. Hines.
  Company H—Captain Rufus A. Barrier.
  Company I—Captain Junius N. Ramsay.
  Company K—Captain Pinckney A. Kennedy.
THIRTY-FIRST NORTH CAROLINA VOLUNTEERS—Colonel John V. Jordan,
Lieutenant-Colonel Charles W. Knight, Major John A. D. McKay.
  Company A—Captain Samuel P. Collins.
  Company B—Captain James T. Bradley.
  Company C—Captain William J. Long.
  Company D—Captain Ruffin L. Bryant.
  Company E—Captain John J. Allison.
  Company F—Captain Stephen W. Morrisett.
  Company G—Captain Isaac Pipkin.
  Company H—Captain John Smith.
  Company I—Captain W. A. Dewar.
  Company K—Captain Joseph Whitty.
FIFTY-FIRST NORTH CAROLINA VOLUNTEERS—Colonel Hector McKethan,
Lieutenant-Colonel Caleb B. Hobson, Major James R. McDonald.
  Company A—Captain Edward Southerland.
  Company B—Captain Walter R. Bell.
  Company C—Captain Samuel M. Stanford.
  Company D—Captain Robert J. McEachan.
  Company E—Captain Willis H. Pope.
  Company F—Captain William S. Norment.
  Company G—Captain James W. Lippett.
  Company H—Captain Samuel W. Maultsby.
  Company I—Captain George Sloan.
  Company K—Captain William J. Murphy.
SIXTY-FIRST NORTH CAROLINA VOLUNTEERS—Colonel James D. Radcliffe,
Lieutenant-Colonel William S. Devane, Major Henry Harding.
  Company A—Captain James H. Robinson.
  Company B—Captain William N. Stevenson.
  Company C—Captain Edward Mallet.
  Company D—Captain Nathan A. Ramsey.
  Company E—Captain William S. Byrd.
  Company F—Captain Andrew J. Moore.
  Company G—Captain Lemuel L. Keith.
  Company H—Captain William B. Lanier.
  Company I—Captain William T. Choat.
  Company K—Captain Samuel W. Noble.

FIRST VOLUNTEER REGIMENT OF GEORGIA—Colonel C. H. Olmsted.

EIGHTEENTH GEORGIA BATTALION (Savannah Volunteer Guards)—Major W. S. Bassinger.

NINETEENTH GEORGIA REGIMENT—Colonel Andrew J. Hutchins.

TWENTY-THIRD GEORGIA REGIMENT—Colonel James H. Huggins; Major M. R. Ballinger.

TWENTY-SEVENTH GEORGIA REGIMENT—Major Gardner.

TWENTY-EIGHTH GEORGIA REGIMENT—Captain W. P. Crawford.

THIRTY-SECOND GEORGIA REGIMENT—Colonel (afterwards Brigadier-General) Geo. P. Harrison, Jr.

These commands were stationed generally on James Island, and detachments from them served at Fort Wagner and Battery Gregg three days at a time.. There were never more than sixteen hundred men on Morris Island at one time; often this force was reduced below one thousand. Just before the evacuation it amounted to but seven hundred and fifty. The artillerists generally served six or seven days before relieved. Every effort has been made to have the list complete and correct. The responses from North Carolina having been most full, the names of company commanders could be given.

CASUALTIES.

COMMANDS.	COMMISSIONED			ENLISTED.			GRAND TOTAL		
	Killed.	Wounded.	Missing.	Killed.	Wounded.	Missing.	Killed.	Wounded.	Missing.
1st South Carolina Infantry...	1	....	....	1	9	1	2	9	1
20th " " " ...	....	....	....	5	18	....	5	18	....
21st " " " ...	2	5	2	13	110	54	15	115	56
25th " " " ...	2	8	....	11	101	10	13	109	10
Charleston Battalion..........	1	7	1	7	39	1	8	46	2
1st South Carolina Artillery...	1	8	....	32	58	62	33	66	62
2d " " " ...	...	....	....	3	3	....	3	3	....
P. B. L. Artillery........ ...	....	....	....	1	....	....	1	....	....
Siege Train.....	....	....	....	1	2	....	1	2	....
Lucas' Battalion Artillery.....	1	1	....	4	27	....	5	28	....
Gist Guard Artillery..........	....	....	....	2	3	....	2	3	....
Matthewes Artillery.........	....	....	....	....	3	....	...	3	....
Marion Artillery.......... ..	....	....	....	....	1	....	....	1	....
7th South Carolina Battalion...	....	....	1	3	....	10	3	....	11
8th North Carolina Troops....	....	1	....	2	17	....	2	18	....
51st " " "	1	5	....	16	55	....	17	60	...
61st " " "	....	....	....	2	2	....	2	2	...
1st Georgia Volunteers.......	1	....	....	2	7	....	3	7	....
18th " "	....	1	....	4	4	....	4	5	....
28th " "	1	1	....	2	21	7	3	22	7
63d " "	....	2	...	4	8	....	2	10	....
32d " "	....	1	....	2	7	....	2	8	....
12th Georgia Battalion	....	....	...	1	4	....	1	4	....
Staff.......................	2	4	...	....	....	....	2	4	....
Totals................	3	44	4	118	499	145	129	543	149

ARMAMENT OF FORT WAGNER, AUGUST 21, 1863.

(Commencing on East, or Sea Face.)

1. 8-inch S. C. Howitzer on curtain, bearing on the land ; in good working order.
2. 10-inch Columbiad on sea face ; unserviceable chassis ; disabled.
3. 10-inch Columbiad on sea face, to bear on beach ; in good working order.
4. 32-pounder Smooth-bore on sea face, to bear on beach ; in good working order.
5. 8-inch Siege Howitzer on land face in salient ; in good working order.
6. 42-pounder Carronade on land face ; in good working order.
7. 8-inch Naval Shell Gun on land face ; in good working order.
8. 32-pounder Smooth-bore on land face ; in good working order.
9. 32-pounder Smooth-bore on land face ; carriage injured, but could be worked.
10. 8-inch Naval Shell Gun on land face ; carriage much injured, but could be worked.
11. 32-pounder Carronade on land face.

12.   32-pounder Carronade on land face.
13.   8-inch Siege Howitzer on land face.
14.   10-inch Mortar at Western gorge.
15.   32-pounder Carronade at Western gorge.
      These last five in good working order.

ARMAMENT OF BATTERY GREGG.

One 10-inch Columbiad.
One 9-inch Dahlgren.
Detachment of Light Artillery.

Garrison—Infantry, 794 ; Artillery, 240 ; Cavalry, 10 ; Sharp-shooters, 14 ;
Total, 1,058.

Every effort has been made to procure a correct roster of
the Engineers, Surgeons, Chaplains, Sharp-Shooters and
Signal Corps serving on Morris Island, but the responses
were so meagre that to avoid an invidious distinction the
partial list is not published.

R. C. GILCHRIST,
Late Major C. S. P. Artillery.